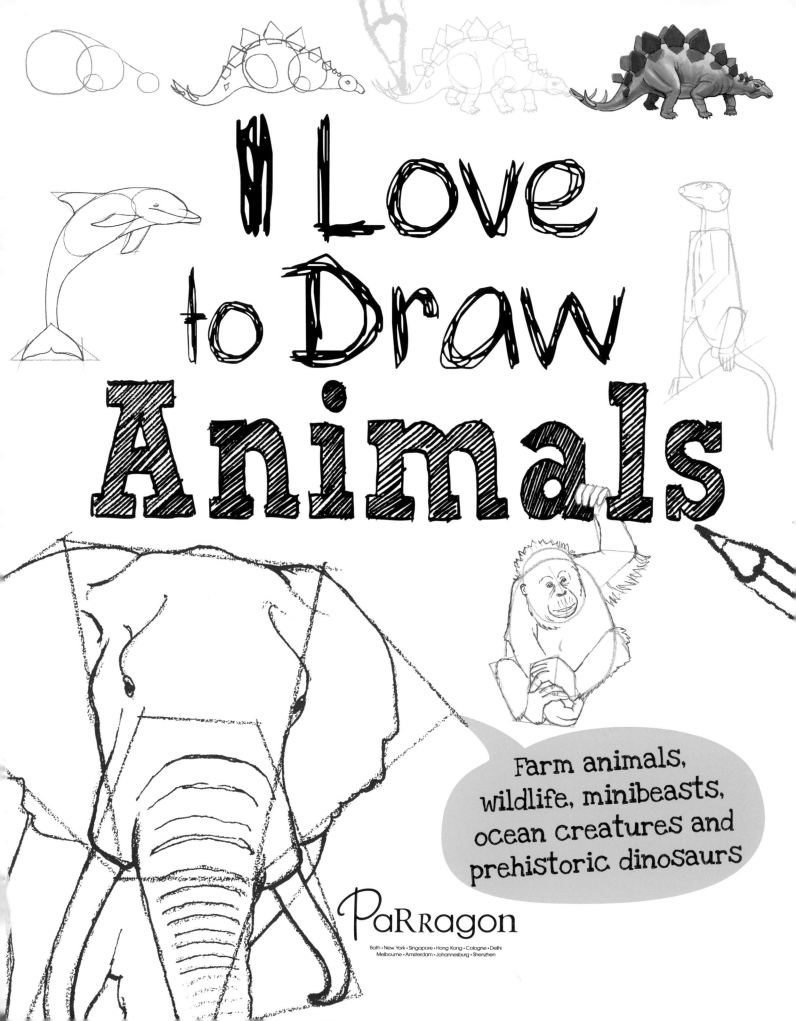

I Love to Draw Animals

Farm animals, wildlife, minibeasts, ocean creatures and prehistoric dinosaurs

PaRRagon

Bath · New York · Singapore · Hong Kong · Cologne · Delhi
Melbourne · Amsterdam · Johannesburg · Shenzhen

This edition published by Parragon in 2013
Parragon
Chartist House
15-17 Trim Street
Bath BA1 1HA, UK
www.parragon.com

Written by; Amanda O'Neill
Illustrated by; Terry Longhurst
Designed by; Chris Scollen and Sarah Williams

ISBN 978-1-4723-1163-4

Printed in China

About this book

Everybody can enjoy drawing, but sometimes it's hard to know where to begin. The subject you want to draw can look very complicated. This book shows you how to start, by breaking down your subject into a series of simple shapes.

The tools you need are very simple. The basic requirements are paper and pencils. Very thin paper wears through if you have to rub out a line, so choose paper that is thick enough to work on. Pencils come with different leads, from very hard to very soft. Very hard (3H) pencils give a clean, thin line, which is best for finishing drawings. Very soft (3B) ones give a thicker, darker line. You will probably find a medium (HB) pencil most useful.

If you want to colour in your drawing, you have the choice of paints, coloured inks or felt-tip pens. Fine felt-tips are useful for drawing outlines, thick felt-tips are better for colouring in.

The most important tool you have is your own eyes. The mistake many people make is to draw what they think something looks like, instead of really looking at it carefully first. Half the secret of making your drawing look good is getting the proportions right. Study your subject before you start and break it down in your mind into sections. Check how much bigger, or longer, or shorter one part is than another. Notice where one part joins another and at what angle. See where there are flowing curves and where there are straight lines.

The step-by-step drawings in this book show you exactly how to do this. Each subject is broken down into easy stages, so you can build up your drawing one piece at a time. Look carefully at each shape before – and after – you draw it. If you find you have drawn it the wrong size or in the wrong place, correct it before you go on. Then the next shape will fit into place and piece by piece you can build up a fantastic picture.

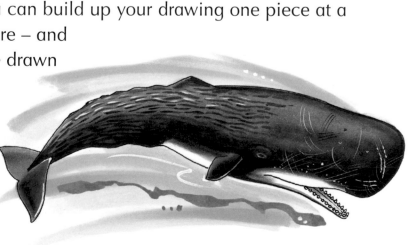

Contents

Stegosaurus

This giant plant-eater was well protected against enemies. It was the size of a tank, armour-plated and armed with a spiked tail. The big upright plates down its back may have been just for display, to make it look even bigger, or they may have been solar panels, to soak up the Sun's heat.

Three circles of different sizes form the heavy body and small head. This little head held a brain the size of a walnut – perhaps the smallest brain of any dinosaur.

1

Join the tops of the two bigger circles to form the arched back. Another small circle forms the top of the front leg.

2

Add a curving line for the tail. Now draw in the shape of the top of the back leg.

3

Finish off the body shape and add the first row of back plates, making them bigger as you go up the body. Shape the head and tail.

4

Long, sharp spikes make the tail a deadly weapon for self-defence.

6

5

Remember to tuck the second row of back plates behind the first.

The legs are short, thick and strong, to carry all that weight. They weren't built for speed.

6

This living tank needs plenty of fuel, so the mouth is large to grab huge mouthfuls of plants.

7

Finish off your outline and draw in creases in the skin at the joints where the legs meet the body.

The name means 'plated reptile'. You can see why from the upright plates down its neck, back and tail.

Tyrannosaurus

Tyrannosaurus was one of the biggest meat-eaters ever to live on Earth. It was so tall that a man would only come up to its knee and it weighed as much as seven cars. It ran on two powerful legs to chase its prey and its mouth was armed with teeth each as long as a man's hand.

1

Make this shape big, for a giant head that could have swallowed you whole!

The circles form the body, which leans forward from its back legs.

2

Link up your head and body with a thick neck. Draw in a long egg shape for the top of the powerful hind leg.

3

This arm section is quite small, for the arms are tiny. But the tail is enormous, to help balance the body.

4

The hind legs are massive and these powerful pillars carry the animal's weight. But the arms are thin and so short that they cannot even reach the mouth.

5 Finish off the head with an eye and two rows of sharp teeth.

6 The useless looking arms end in hands with long clawed fingers.

7 Finish off your outline. The hind feet stand on three strong toes with large claws.

The name means 'tyrant reptile'. A tyrant is a cruel ruler and the other dinosaurs on which Tyrannosaurus preyed must have found that it really lived up to its name.

Triceratops

Despite its fearsome appearance, Triceratops was a harmless plant-eater. The huge horns that give it its name ('three-horned face') were for defence, not attack. The huge, bony frill behind its head was also for protection, guarding its neck from attack from behind.

1 Start with the body and draw two smaller ovals for the tops of the legs.

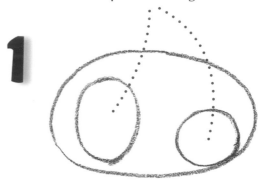

2 The unusual shape of the head includes the neck-frill.

3 Triceratops' head, including the bony neck-frill, was about the size of a door.

The legs are thick and strong – Triceratops weighed as much as two elephants.

4 Add a line for the tail and sketch in the two legs on the other side of the body.

Dinosaurs

5

Complete the basic shape. The head ends in a sharp, bony beak, to bite through the stems of tough plants.

The back edge of the neck-frill is covered with bony knobs.

The outline of the huge body and massive legs is now almost complete.

6

Finish the outline using a slightly wavy line along the back to indicate scales on the skin.

7

Triceratops was the largest of the family of horned dinosaurs, the smallest of which were about the size of pigs. The size of the horns and neck frills varied from species to species.

Broad feet end in stubby toes with strong toenails.

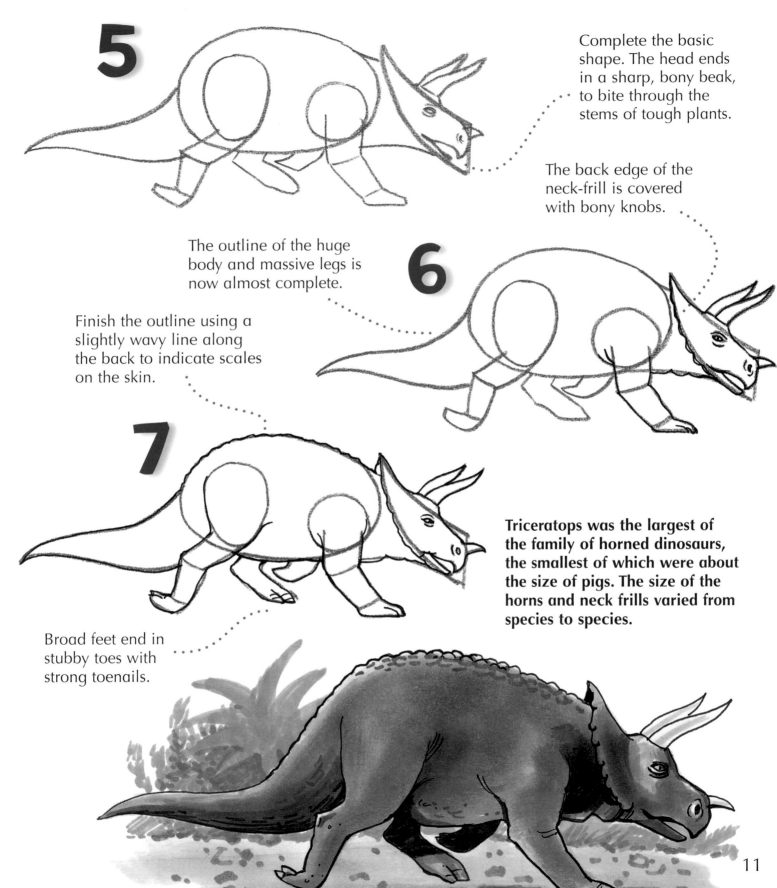

11

Pteranodon

When dinosaurs ruled the earth, flying reptiles, or pterosaurs, ruled the skies. They came in many shapes and sizes. Some were as small as sparrows, but Pteranodon was a giant, about the size of a glider. In fact, scientists think it flew by gliding – it was probably too big to flap its wings.

These two shapes will form the body and hind legs.

1

The head, with its open jaws, will fit into this long box shape.

2

A long, bony crest probably helped to balance the heavy head in flight.

3

The legs are tiny – not the legs of a creature that does much walking.

Add the first wing. It is made of leathery skin attached to the arm and finger bones.

4

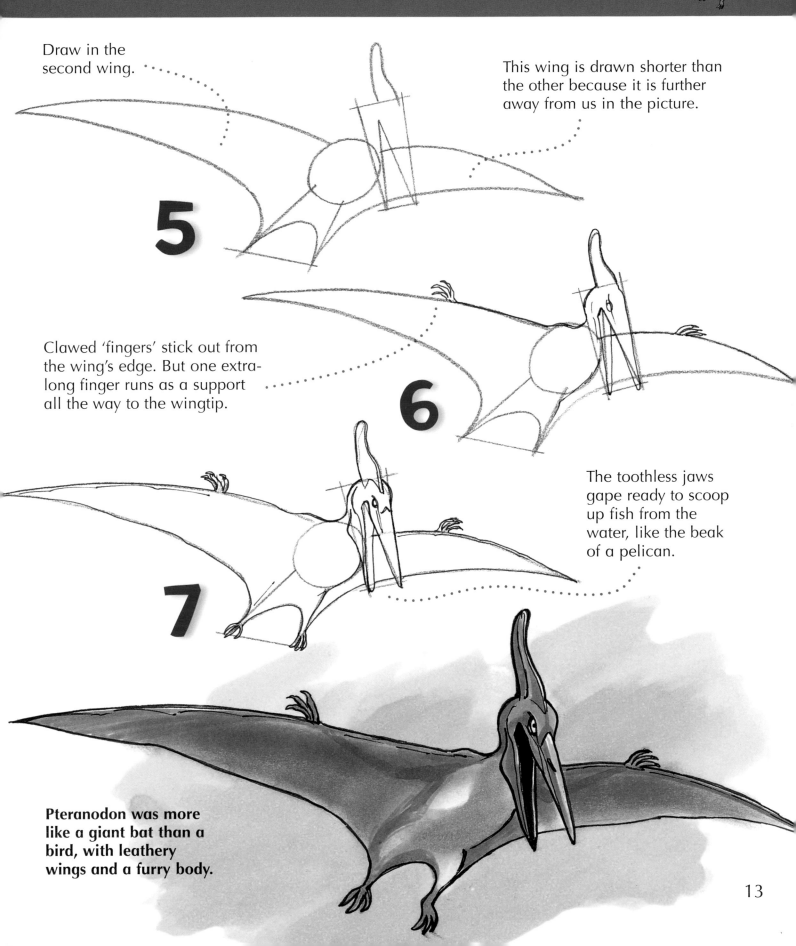

Draw in the second wing.

This wing is drawn shorter than the other because it is further away from us in the picture.

5

Clawed 'fingers' stick out from the wing's edge. But one extra-long finger runs as a support all the way to the wingtip.

6

7

The toothless jaws gape ready to scoop up fish from the water, like the beak of a pelican.

Pteranodon was more like a giant bat than a bird, with leathery wings and a furry body.

Diplodocus

Diplodocus was not the biggest dinosaur, but it was one of the longest. It was as long as a tennis court, though most of its length was neck and tail. It was built like a suspension bridge, with its long body supported on column-like legs.

1 Start with head and body shapes. The head is tiny compared to the body – in fact, it was hardly bigger than a modern horse's head.

2 Draw a medium-sized oval below the head as a guideline for the curve of the neck.

Now draw the neck around your oval.

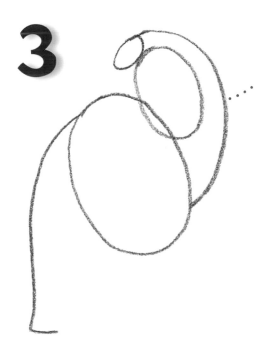

3

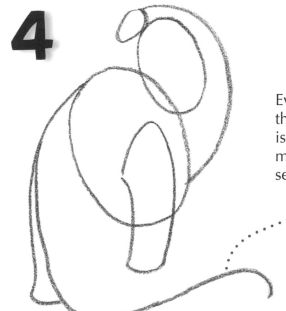

4 Even longer than the neck, the tail is made up of more than 70 separate bones.

5

The long neck had muscles like the steel cables of a crane, to help lift the head.

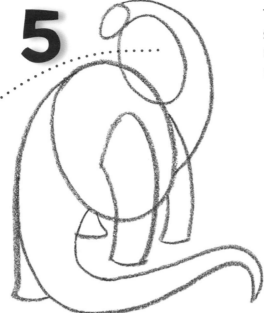

The jaws had teeth only at the front, to strip leaves from branches. Diplodocus must have spent its whole life eating, as it needed lots of food to survive.

6

7

Ink in your outlines, adding shading to give weight to the huge legs and tail.

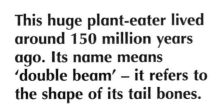

This huge plant-eater lived around 150 million years ago. Its name means 'double beam' – it refers to the shape of its tail bones.

15

Deinonychus

Deinonychus means 'terrible claw' and the long claw on its hind foot was a truly terrible weapon. The clawed toe operated on a special hinge to slash down like a knife. This meat-eater was quite small for a dinosaur – not much taller than a man. It probably hunted in packs to tackle large prey.

1

Two ovals form the head and body.

2

Draw another oval within the body to make the top of the hind leg, taking up about half of the space.

You need a surprisingly long, flowing line for the tail.

3

The hind leg is long and strong, helping Deinonychus to run fast after its prey.

4

The skull is quite large and heavy for such a small dinosaur.

The tail stands out stiffly behind the body to keep Deinonychus perfectly balanced while running.

5

Strong arms with three long, clawed fingers are designed for grabbing prey.

The 'terrible claw' is held high above the two walking claws. This saves it from being worn down and blunted by scraping on the ground.

Tidy up the shape of the head and put some teeth in that big mouth.

The raised back leg flows smoothly from the oval of the thigh.

6

7

The outline is complete and ready to fill in.

A streamlined build and long legs made Deinonychus both swift and agile. It also had quite a large brain, making it a crafty hunter. Slow, lumbering grass-eaters stood little chance of escape!

17

Cow

Dairy cows provide us with milk, which is used to make butter and cheese. There are various breeds, most easily told apart by the colour. The big, black and white Friesian is one of the most common.

1

Begin with these two four-sided shapes. Note that the head is so much smaller than the deep body.

The triangle forms the deep chest and top of the leg.

2

Remember to set the small oval (which will become the knee) close to the chest. This will ensure that the forelegs are in the right position.

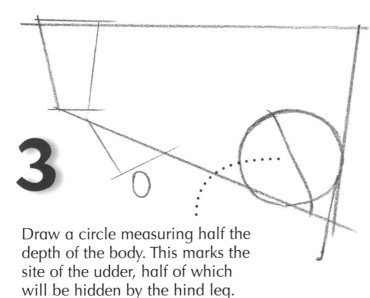

3

Draw a circle measuring half the depth of the body. This marks the site of the udder, half of which will be hidden by the hind leg.

The forelegs are quite straight, but the short, strong hind legs are slightly slanted. The front feet are level with each other, but one hind foot is drawn slightly forward to support the weight of the body.

4

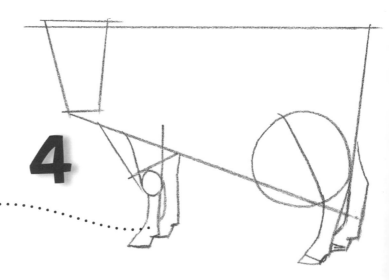

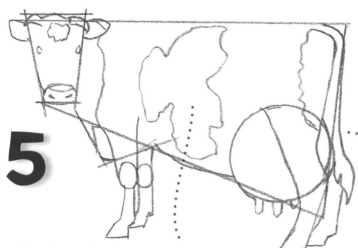

5

The tail hangs straight down like an old-fashioned bell rope, with a silky tuft at the end.

Sketch in the black and white markings. They can be any shape you like – no two cows are marked exactly alike.

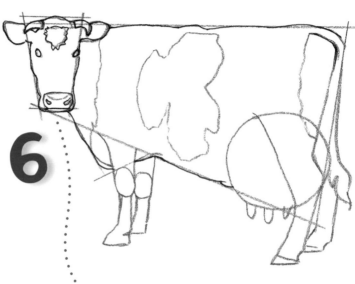

6

Add details of the face, spacing the eyes and ears well apart. Decide whether your cow has horns – many breeds are born hornless ('polled') or have their horns removed.

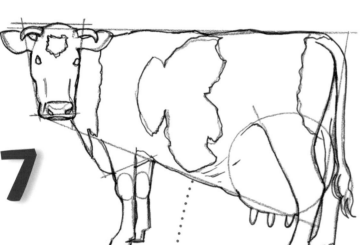

7

Start tidying up the outline and add final details. The line of the chest and underside needs to be worked on carefully.

There's a good reason why the cow's body is so large. It houses four stomachs to help the cow process enormous amounts of food and drink. In a single week an adult cow can eat her own weight in grass!

Chicken

Fifty years ago, every farmyard had a flock of chickens pecking around to provide eggs and meat. Today, hens are often kept indoors in huge 'factory' farms. But some farms keep 'free range' chickens outdoors where they can enjoy fresh air and space.

Naturally, the chicken starts with an egg! This egg shape will become its body.

1

2

Add a curving line for the neck and a much smaller egg for the head.

Complete the neck and add the comb (the fleshy growth, like a crest, on top of the head).

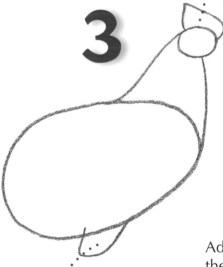

3

The top of the leg will be covered in feathers when the drawing is complete.

Add tail and legs and the chicken begins to appear. Don't put the legs too far forward!

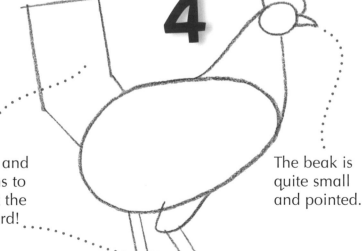

4

The beak is quite small and pointed.

5

Fill in some detail. Bring the head to life by adding the eye and the wattle (another fleshy growth hanging below the beak). Sketch in wings and toes.

6

The comb has a jagged edge – like the teeth of a hair-comb.

Now you can add some form to the wings.

7

A chicken has several thousand feathers, but you don't need to draw all of them! Instead, suggest a feathery texture with a little shading.

21

Horse

In your great-grandparents' day, horses were very important on the farm. Horse power was the only power available for ploughing, harrowing, carting and other heavy work. Today, they have been replaced by machinery and are mostly kept just for riding.

1

Take care with the spacing of the first two shapes.

The top of this oval needs to be a little lower than the shield-like shapes on either side.

2

Complete the neck and back. Add a circle at the point where the foreleg will begin.

3

Three more lines running from the head circle give the shape of the muzzle.

Horses have bony legs with knobbly knees. Mark out the position of the leg joints with small rounded shapes. Sketch in the tail.

4

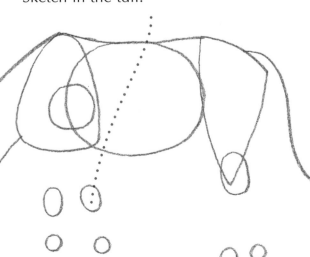

22

5

When the legs are added, body and legs form a rough square. If it's a rectangle, either the body or the legs are too long! Draw in the face, ears and mane, and add some shape to the tail.

6

The long, strong neck is heavily muscled. A line down the throat will show you where to add shading.

7

Finish off your outline. Now it really begins to look like a horse. This one is eating grass, so draw the mouth slightly open.

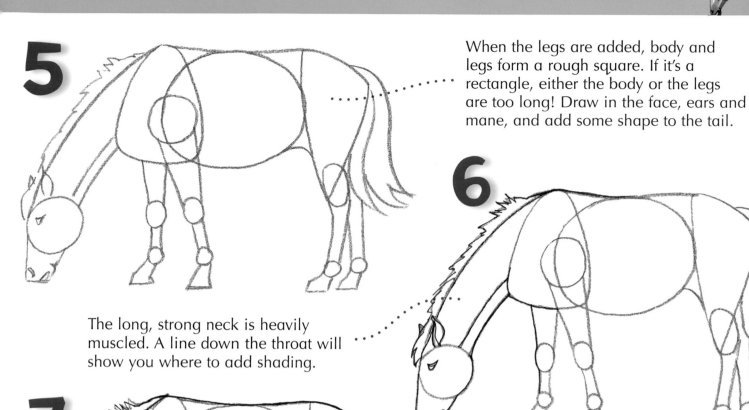

Horses come in a wonderful range of colours – black, grey, all shades of brown or even spotted – the choice is yours. You may like to add markings such as a tar or blaze on the face, or white 'stockings'.

Pig

There is an old saying that every part of the pig can be used except its squeal! As well as meat, pigs provide leather and even bristles for brushes. They were once also valued as bulldozers to clear rough land, grubbing up roots and plants with their snouts.

We say 'as fat as a pig', so start with two fat circles.

1

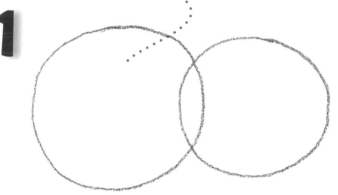

This looks more complicated than it is! Add two more simple shapes to create the head and the top of a front leg.

2

Pop on a pair of ears and suddenly the shapes start to make sense. Level off the back and add a curve at the rear for the top of the second hindleg.

3

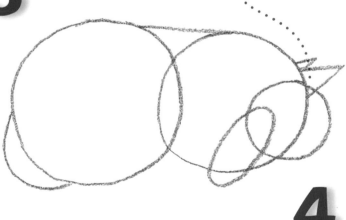

4

Two more additions make your sketch much more piggy. Put in the tops of the legs and draw a nose. This snout turns up like a little teapot spout.

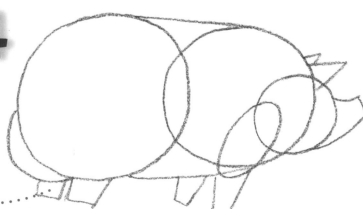

5

6 Now you can add a few details. Place the small eye just in front of the ears, level with the tip of the snout.

With completed legs and a loosely curled tail, the pig's outline is all there. Round off the belly in front of the hind leg.

7

Your pig is ready for you to finish off the outline.

Pigs don't have to be pink! Some breeds are black, some ginger, some spotted and some (Saddlebacks) have a white band across a dark body. In fact, pink pigs have a problem – like us, they can suffer from sunburn in the summer!

On the Farm

Sheepdog

It takes a special kind of dog to control several hundred sheep. The clever, tireless Border Collie was made for the job. He is so keen on herding that if he has no sheep to work, he will round up chickens in the farmyard or even members of his human 'family'.

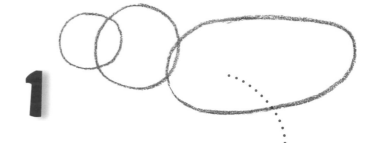

1 These three rounded shapes form the head, neck and powerful body of your sheepdog.

Join the neck to the body and mark out the shapes, which will form the hindquarters and curling tail.

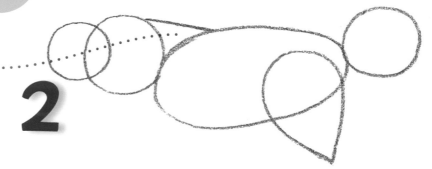

2

3

Pricked ears and a long muzzle help to give a keen expression. Add a small oval, which will be a foreleg joint.

Start to draw in the legs to suggest that the sheepdog is slightly crouched as it runs.

The tail swirls upward at the end and fits within the circle you have already drawn.

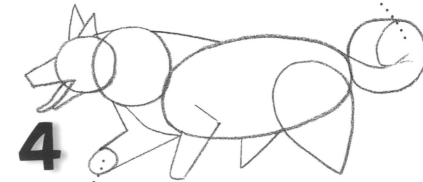

4

5

A sheepdog runs many miles in a working day. He keeps his feet low as he runs, to save energy, in a smooth, fast gallop.

Finish off the legs and complete the face by adding an eye.

Start to draw in more detail and give your outlines a soft edge to look like fur. The neck is quite long, strong, muscular and slightly arched.

6

This collie has a thick, weatherproof coat. Draw in fringes at the back of the legs and make the tail bushy.

7

Add wavy lines to show where your sheepdog will have patches of black and white in his fur.

Most Border Collies are black and white. They are not supposed to have too much white on them – farmers used to believe that sheep would ignore a white dog, thinking it was just another sheep!

27

Tiger

The tiger is a large and powerful predator, which usually hunts by stealth at night. It feeds mainly on wild oxen and buffalo, which it kills with a bite to the back of the neck or the throat. Tigers are found in south and south-east Asia.

Start with these three simple shapes. Pay attention to their sizes and the space between them.

1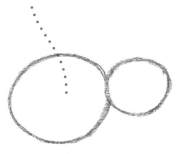

Add the flowing shape of the body, the curved tail and the outstretched foreleg.

2

Start to draw in the rear legs.

Add this shape for the tiger's snout.

3

The front leg is strong and powerful at the shoulder, which is represented by the centre circle.

The tail trails out behind the tiger.

This leg is centred under the shoulder. It is about as long as the body is deep.

4

All of the tiger's weight is on one foreleg. Draw the two back legs in this way. They appear smaller as they are further away from us.

Begin to add details for the eyes, mouth and the striped coat.

The nose, mouth and eye bring the head to life.

5

The underside is paler than the back and without stripes.

Begin to define the tiger's shape with ink.

6

The dark stripes break up the tiger's solid outline.

7

The strong colours of the tiger's coat, its stripes and paler underside are valuable camouflage when it hides in long grass, patiently stalking its prey.

Crocodile

Crocodiles belong to an ancient family, dating back to the time of the dinosaurs. They live mostly in tropical rivers and lakes and are beautifully adapted to a life in the water, although they also like to bask in the Sun on shore.

1

Start with these two simple egg-like shapes for the head and body.

Now add the long, thick tail. This is a useful weapon to stun prey, as well as a swimming aid.

2

Lengthen the head with a long snout, making the head and snout together the same length as the body.

This oval forms the top section of the front leg. It is set upright at the shoulder.

Draw an oval, slanted at an angle, for the upper hind leg.

Two more shapes form the hind leg and foot.

3

Now sketch in the foreleg. The legs are short and quite weak. They are used to crawl on land and are folded close to the body when the crocodile swims.

4

30

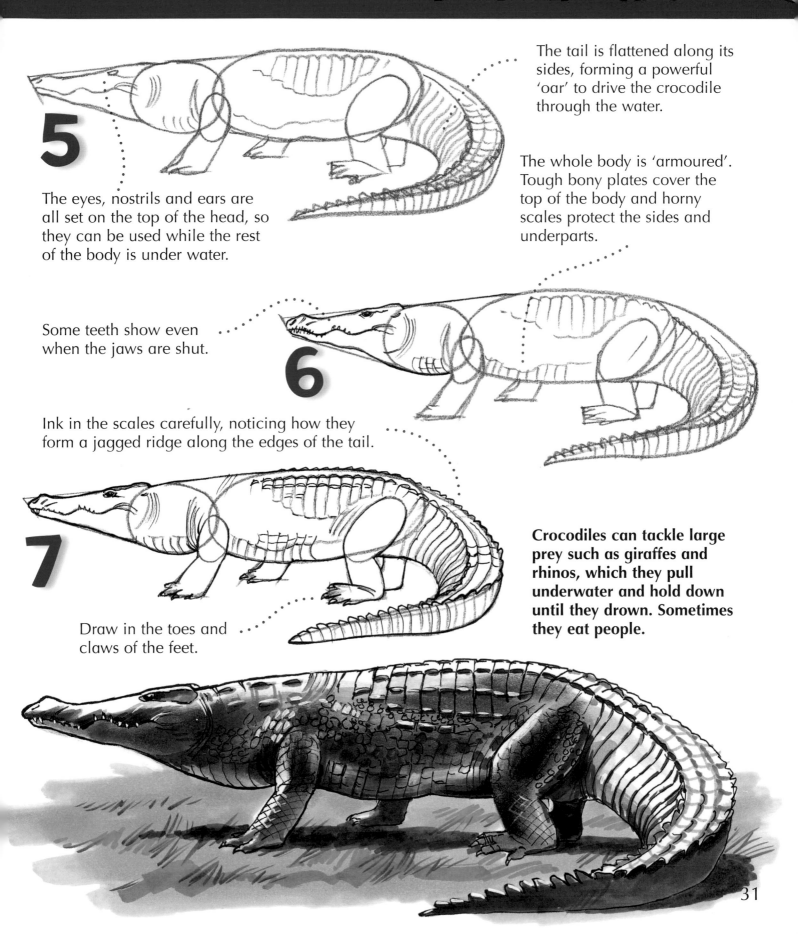

5

The tail is flattened along its sides, forming a powerful 'oar' to drive the crocodile through the water.

The eyes, nostrils and ears are all set on the top of the head, so they can be used while the rest of the body is under water.

The whole body is 'armoured'. Tough bony plates cover the top of the body and horny scales protect the sides and underparts.

Some teeth show even when the jaws are shut.

6

Ink in the scales carefully, noticing how they form a jagged ridge along the edges of the tail.

7

Crocodiles can tackle large prey such as giraffes and rhinos, which they pull underwater and hold down until they drown. Sometimes they eat people.

Draw in the toes and claws of the feet.

Gorilla

Gorillas are the biggest and heaviest of the apes. In the forests of tropical Africa, they live in family groups headed by big males, who develop silver coloured backs with age. These gentle giants feed on leaves and shoots, but are too heavy to climb trees.

1 Start with a big oval for the head and add a second, smaller oval beside it.

2 Now draw a third oval. Most of this drawing is made up of these shapes. This helps to give the impression of great masses of muscle.

Add a fourth oval, a little way below your first group. This will become an arm.

3 Another oval, as big as the head, forms the muscular hindquarters.

Now you can start joining up your pattern of ovals, keeping your lines smooth.

Two curving lines link the arm to the shoulder. The arms are very powerful and thicker than a human body-builder's.

When you add the other, massive foreleg, suddenly the gorilla starts to take shape.

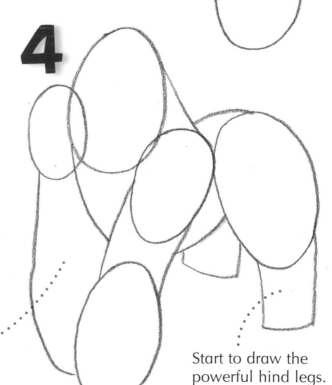

4 Start to draw the powerful hind legs.

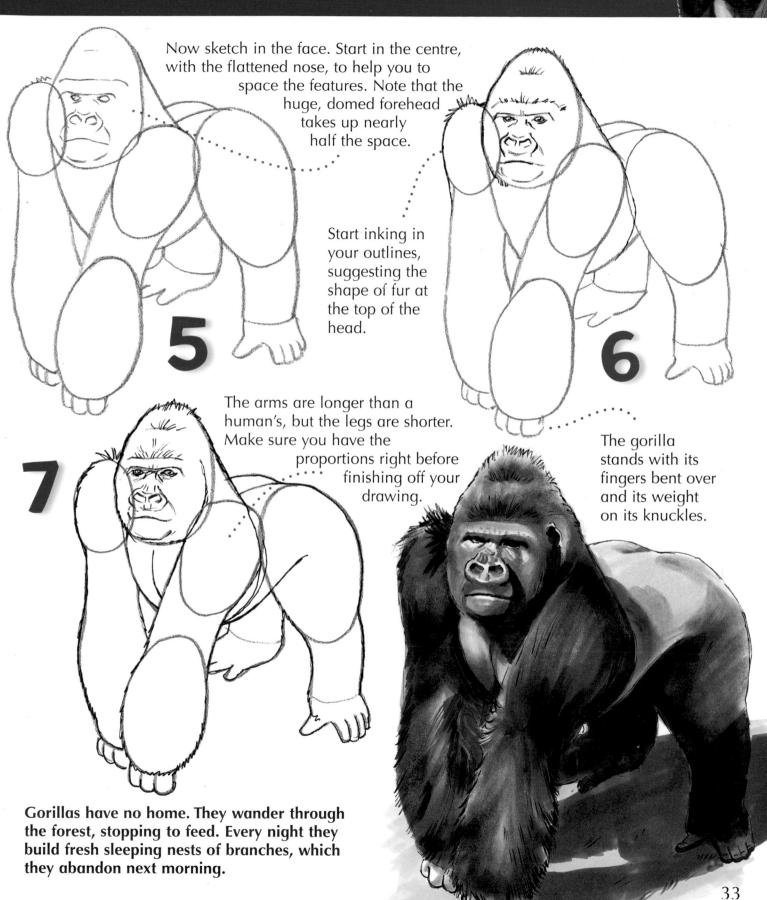

Now sketch in the face. Start in the centre, with the flattened nose, to help you to space the features. Note that the huge, domed forehead takes up nearly half the space.

5

Start inking in your outlines, suggesting the shape of fur at the top of the head.

6

7

The arms are longer than a human's, but the legs are shorter. Make sure you have the proportions right before finishing off your drawing.

The gorilla stands with its fingers bent over and its weight on its knuckles.

Gorillas have no home. They wander through the forest, stopping to feed. Every night they build fresh sleeping nests of branches, which they abandon next morning.

33

Meerkat

This little mongoose is found in the grasslands and deserts of southern Africa. It lives in large family groups, which work together to keep family members fed and safe. Males take turns at sentry duty. Standing upright on a tree or rock, they watch for danger.

1

This shape – like an egg flattened at the top – forms the long, narrow head with its pointed snout.

Copy this shape carefully. It forms guidelines for the upright body, all four legs and even the branch on which the meerkat sentry perches.

2

Now add a neck and draw a long sausage-shape for the body. Make sure this runs down the outline at the back, but leave a gap at the front and a larger one at the base.

Draw the first foreleg, hanging down. It is shaped very much like a human arm, with dangling hands.

This small shape will form the top of a hind leg. The legs are strong enough for the Meerkat to stand up erect for long periods.

3

Now follow the front edge of your guideline to mark out the far shoulder and second foreleg.

4

Two bold curving lines form the second hind leg. Finish it off with a long foot.

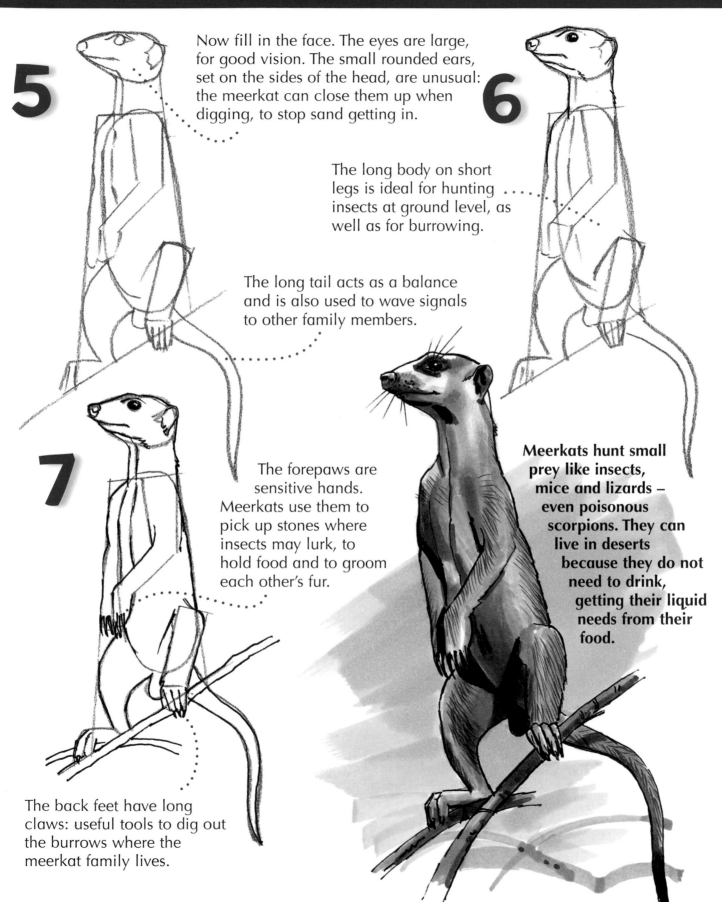

5

Now fill in the face. The eyes are large, for good vision. The small rounded ears, set on the sides of the head, are unusual: the meerkat can close them up when digging, to stop sand getting in.

6

The long body on short legs is ideal for hunting insects at ground level, as well as for burrowing.

The long tail acts as a balance and is also used to wave signals to other family members.

7

The forepaws are sensitive hands. Meerkats use them to pick up stones where insects may lurk, to hold food and to groom each other's fur.

The back feet have long claws: useful tools to dig out the burrows where the meerkat family lives.

Meerkats hunt small prey like insects, mice and lizards – even poisonous scorpions. They can live in deserts because they do not need to drink, getting their liquid needs from their food.

35

Orangutan

Found only on the south-east Asian islands of Borneo and Sumatra, this giant ape lives in the trees. It feeds on leaves, fruit and flowers, and spends most of its life high above the ground. The world's largest tree-living mammal, it has long, strong arms to pull it through the branches.

1

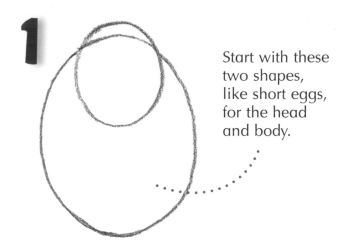

Start with these two shapes, like short eggs, for the head and body.

This shape will form the rounded muzzle.

2

Build this shape with four lines joined to the base of your big oval. It will form the folded limbs.

Divide the face down the centre as a guideline to help you position the eyes and nose.

3

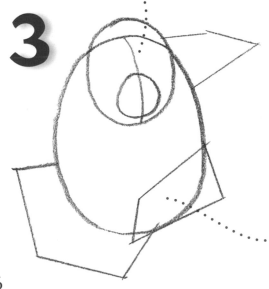

Draw the raised arm and hand in three sections. Orangutans have unusually long arms, to help them climb.

Add a four-sided shape for one bent back leg, just overlapping the other 'leg' shape.

4

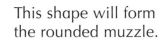
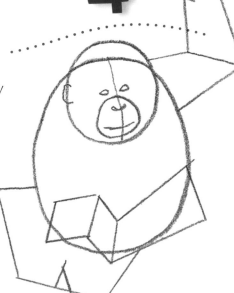

Draw a hand like your own – only bigger and much more powerful.

5

Sketch in the coarse, shaggy coat, which hangs in 'sleeves' from the arms. Orangutans have the longest hair of any ape.

6

The short, bandy legs are used for walking – but, with double-jointed hips, they are even more useful as a second pair of 'arms', complete with finger-like toes.

Now draw in the details of the face, with its broad nose and deep-set eyes.

Strengthen the outlines ready for colouring.

7

At night, Orangutans build nests in the forks of trees, bending branches to make a secure platform.

'Orangutan' is a Malay word meaning 'man of the forest'. Apes and humans belong to the same family and some scientists believe the Orangutan is our nearest relative.

Wild Animals

Elephant

The African Elephant is the largest living land mammal. It can weigh as much as seven cars. Even a baby elephant weighs as much as a fully grown man. Asian Elephants are smaller than their African cousins, though they are still huge animals.

1

Draw this four-sided shape for the head, with triangles on either side for ears. Huge ears show that this is an African Elephant – Asian Elephants have smaller ears.

Add another uneven four-sided shape below. This does not form part of your finished drawing, but acts as a guideline for the position of the tusks.

2

Draw this heavy column below the head. The front legs will fit into this shape.

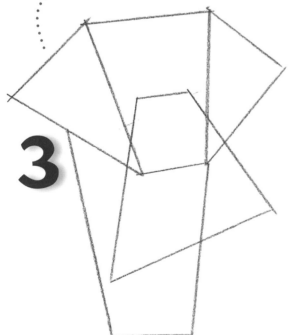

3

Now you can start shaping your elephant, adding the massive legs, the long trunk and curving the body behind the head.

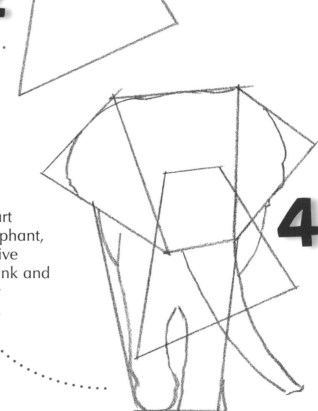

4

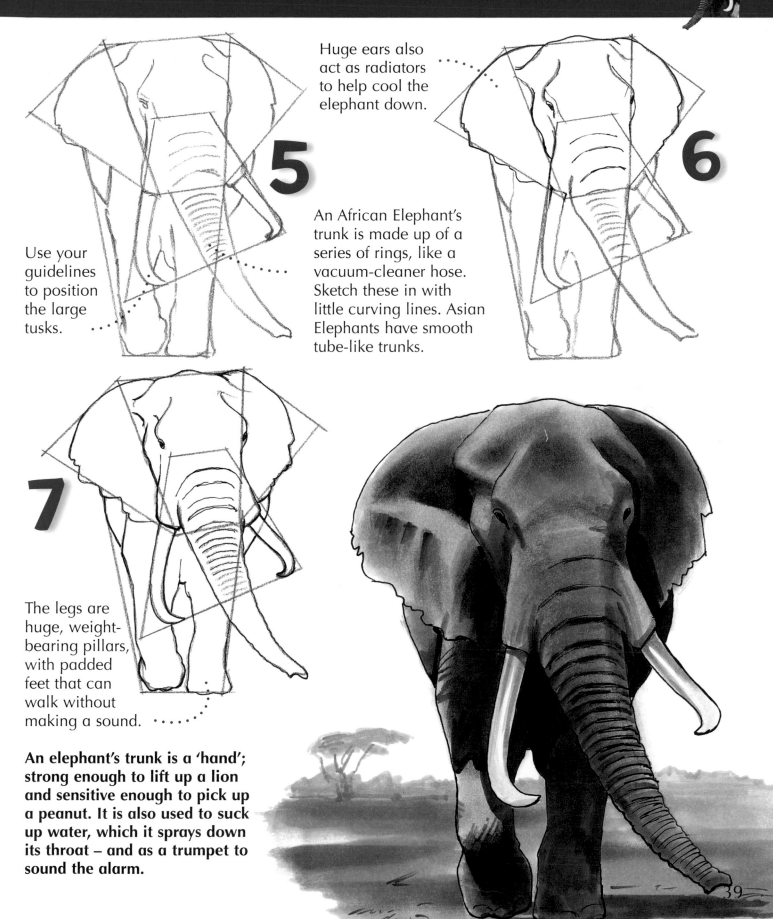

5

Use your guidelines to position the large tusks.

Huge ears also act as radiators to help cool the elephant down.

6

An African Elephant's trunk is made up of a series of rings, like a vacuum-cleaner hose. Sketch these in with little curving lines. Asian Elephants have smooth tube-like trunks.

7

The legs are huge, weight-bearing pillars, with padded feet that can walk without making a sound.

An elephant's trunk is a 'hand'; strong enough to lift up a lion and sensitive enough to pick up a peanut. It is also used to suck up water, which it sprays down its throat – and as a trumpet to sound the alarm.

39

Ocean Animals

Dolphin

The Dolphin is the acrobat of the ocean. Some species can leap as high as 7 metres (twice the height of an elephant) out of the water – and perform somersaults in mid-air.

1 Draw two ovals for the head and body.

2 Dolphins are very intelligent – the large head houses a big brain.

A large triangle forms the tail.

3 Now join the tail to the body in a graceful curve.

Add a triangle for this fin.

4 Now start to shape the tail.

The flippers are quite short.

The long jaw is called a beak.

40

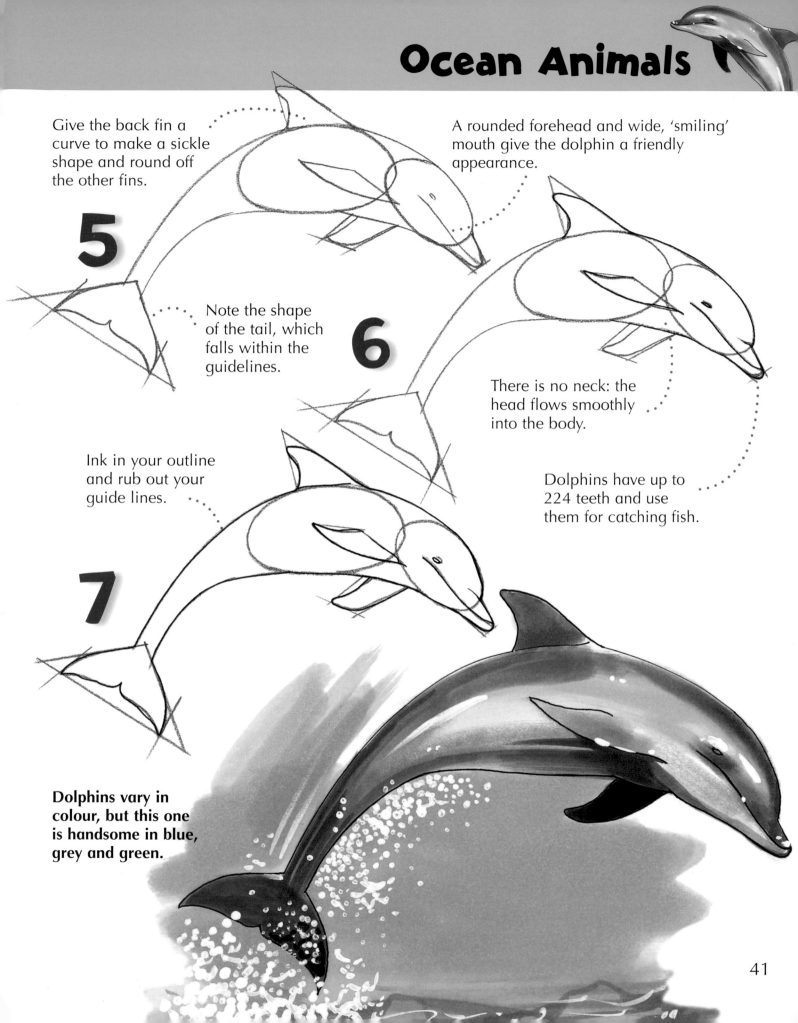

Give the back fin a curve to make a sickle shape and round off the other fins.

5

A rounded forehead and wide, 'smiling' mouth give the dolphin a friendly appearance.

Note the shape of the tail, which falls within the guidelines.

6

There is no neck: the head flows smoothly into the body.

Ink in your outline and rub out your guide lines.

Dolphins have up to 224 teeth and use them for catching fish.

7

Dolphins vary in colour, but this one is handsome in blue, grey and green.

41

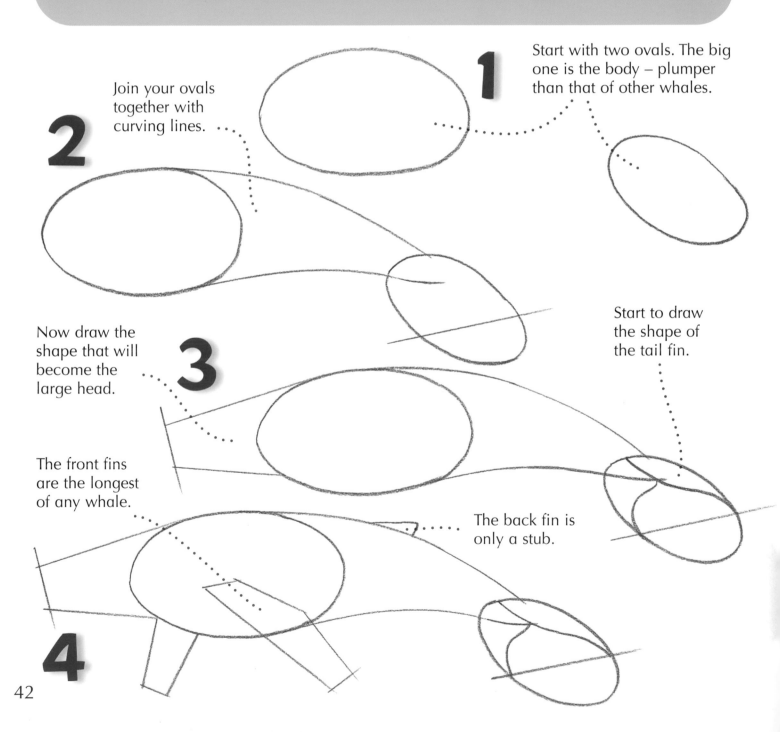

Ocean Animals

Humpback Whale

Humpback Whales are famous for their 'songs'. They 'talk' to each other underwater in musical-sounding clicks. Despite its large size, the Humpback feeds only on tiny sea creatures. A built-in sieve at the back of its mouth allows it to filter these out from mouthfuls of seawater.

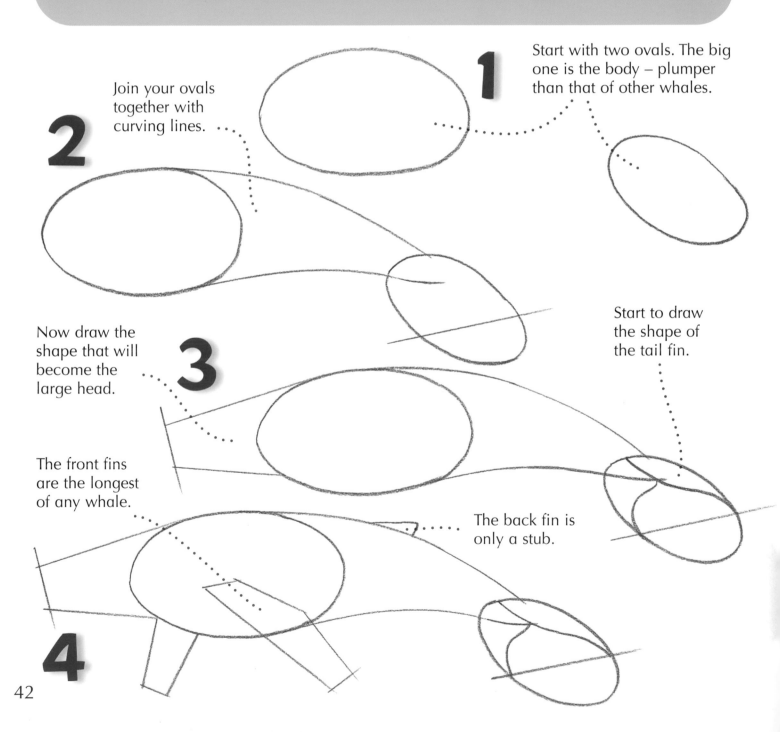

1 Start with two ovals. The big one is the body – plumper than that of other whales.

2 Join your ovals together with curving lines.

3 Now draw the shape that will become the large head.

Start to draw the shape of the tail fin.

4 The front fins are the longest of any whale.

The back fin is only a stub.

42

The small eye is set well back in the head.

Start to add more detail and smooth off the outline to your drawing.

5

Shape the fins, with a wavy front edge.

The tail is large – from tip to tip, larger than an elephant!

6

Deep grooves in the throat stretch like elastic when the whale is feeding.

The rounded back gives the Humpback its name.

7

Complete your drawing and it is ready to colour in.

Humpbacks live in family groups, which travel together for thousands of miles across the oceans.

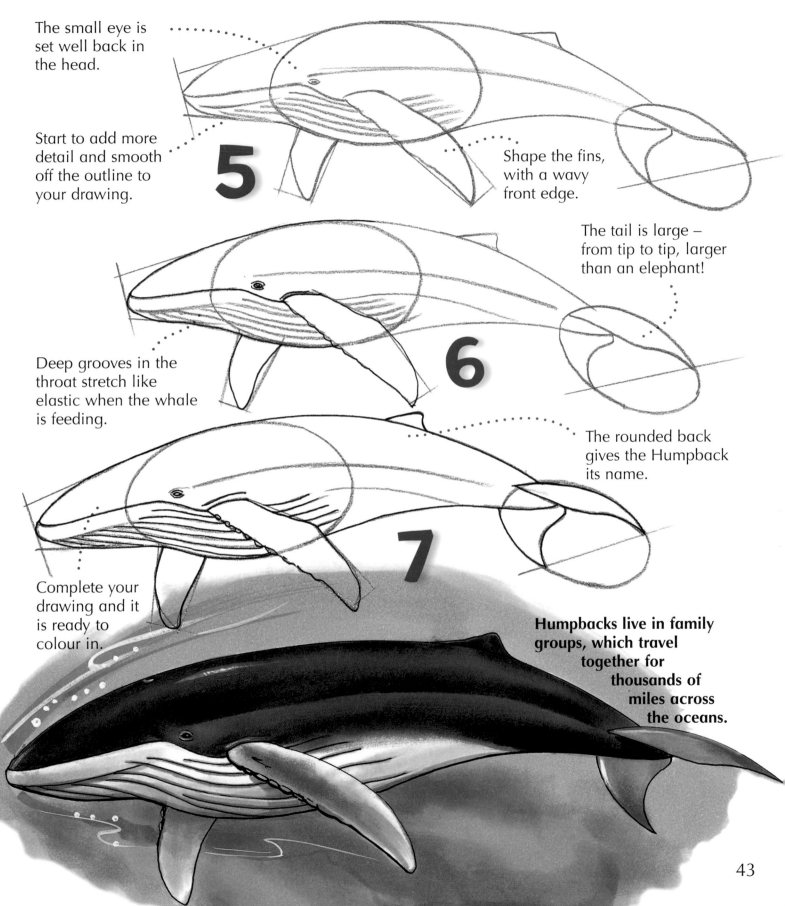

Great White Shark

This is the biggest and most dangerous of all sharks. It hunts large prey like seals and dolphins – and sometimes attacks humans. Most people know this shark best as the giant man-eater in the film Jaws.

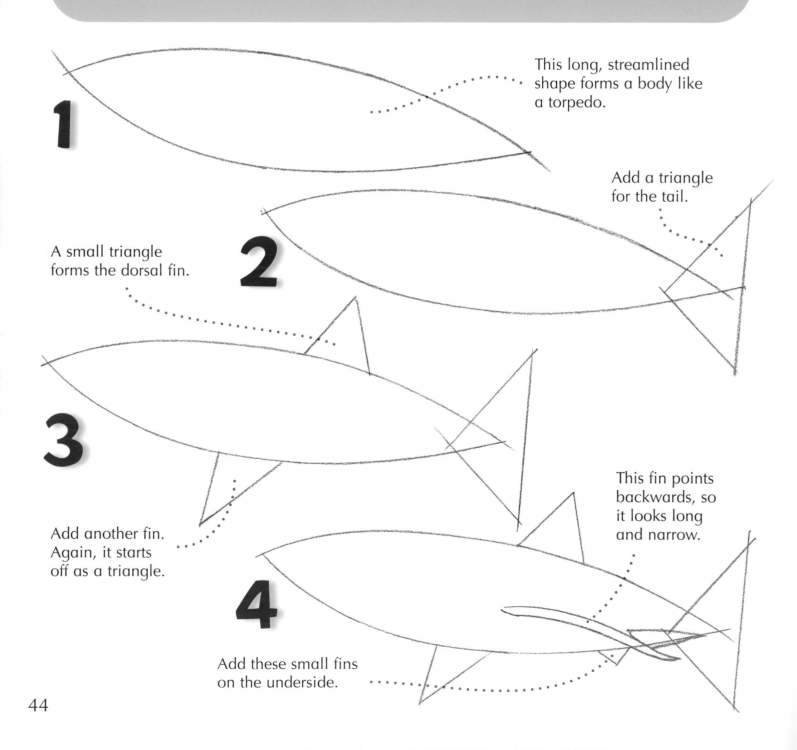

1

This long, streamlined shape forms a body like a torpedo.

2

Add a triangle for the tail.

A small triangle forms the dorsal fin.

3

This fin points backwards, so it looks long and narrow.

Add another fin. Again, it starts off as a triangle.

4

Add these small fins on the underside.

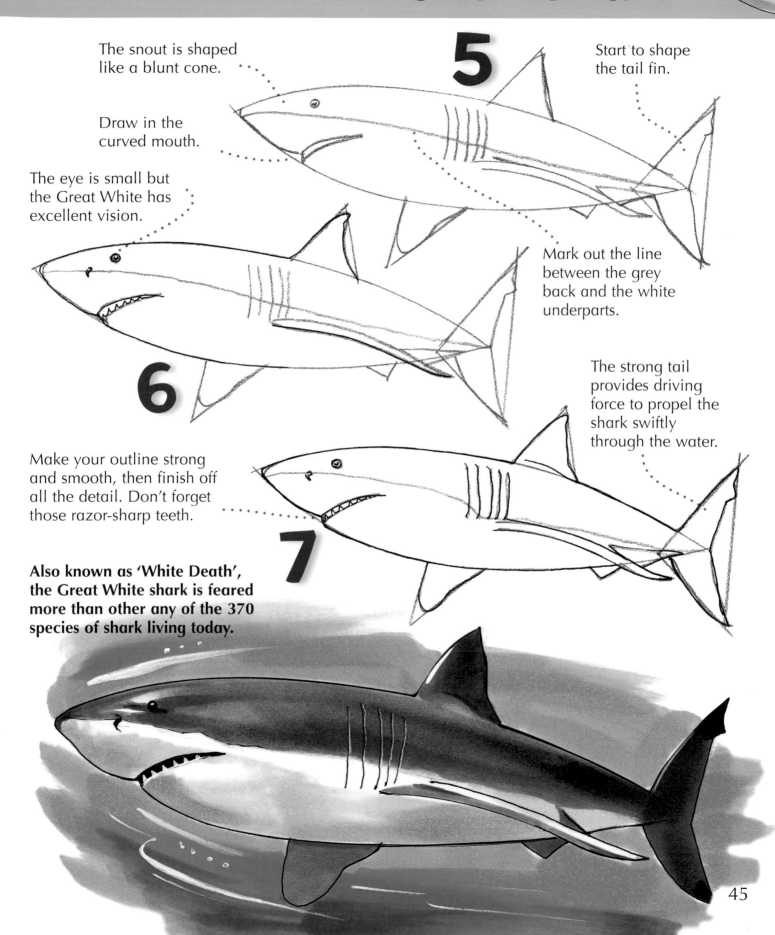

The snout is shaped like a blunt cone.

5

Start to shape the tail fin.

Draw in the curved mouth.

The eye is small but the Great White has excellent vision.

6

Mark out the line between the grey back and the white underparts.

The strong tail provides driving force to propel the shark swiftly through the water.

Make your outline strong and smooth, then finish off all the detail. Don't forget those razor-sharp teeth.

7

Also known as 'White Death', the Great White shark is feared more than other any of the 370 species of shark living today.

Killer Whale

The Killer Whale, also known as an Orca, is not actually a whale at all, but a member of the dolphin family. Large groups of Orcas hunt in fierce packs to attack seals, porpoises and even whales. But tame Orcas have shown themselves to be as intelligent and friendly as more popular dolphins.

1

Start with a large oval for the body.

A smaller, tilted oval marks out the tail.

2

Add a large, boxy shape for the head.

Now attach the tail to the body with a curving line.

3

Cut off the corners of the head shape, but leave it blunt.

The back fin is the tallest of any sea mammal – it stands as high as a man.

Add a graceful curve to form the underside of the Orca and draw a line to mark where the tail will end.

4

Draw an oval to form this flipper.

46

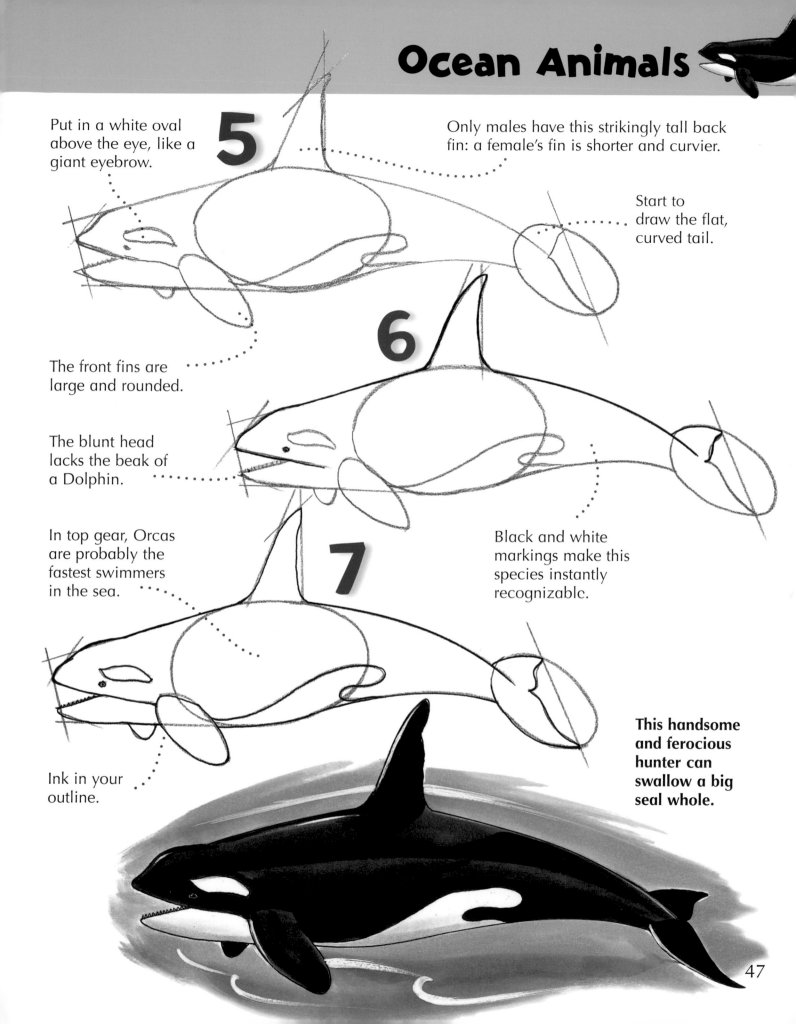

5

Put in a white oval above the eye, like a giant eyebrow.

Only males have this strikingly tall back fin: a female's fin is shorter and curvier.

Start to draw the flat, curved tail.

The front fins are large and rounded.

6

The blunt head lacks the beak of a Dolphin.

In top gear, Orcas are probably the fastest swimmers in the sea.

7

Black and white markings make this species instantly recognizable.

Ink in your outline.

This handsome and ferocious hunter can swallow a big seal whole.

Hammerhead Shark

You only have to look at a Hammerhead to see how it got its name. The strange, flattened head extends on either side to form a shape just like a hammer.

1 Start with a lopsided crescent, which will become the shark's body.

2 Add another sail-like shape to mark out the position of the tail.

Note how the curved body fits together with the tail.

Draw in curved lines for the strange head.

The upper part of the tail fin is much longer than the lower section.

Start to shape the tail fin.

3

Draw in the 'hammer'. The round eye is placed right at the end, giving good vision to one side.

4

Draw triangles for the fins.

A curved line here marks where the white of the underparts begins.

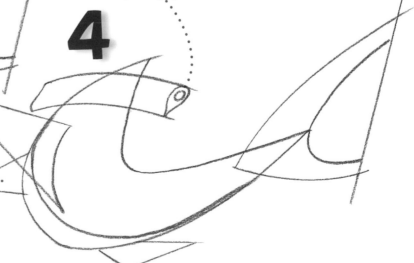

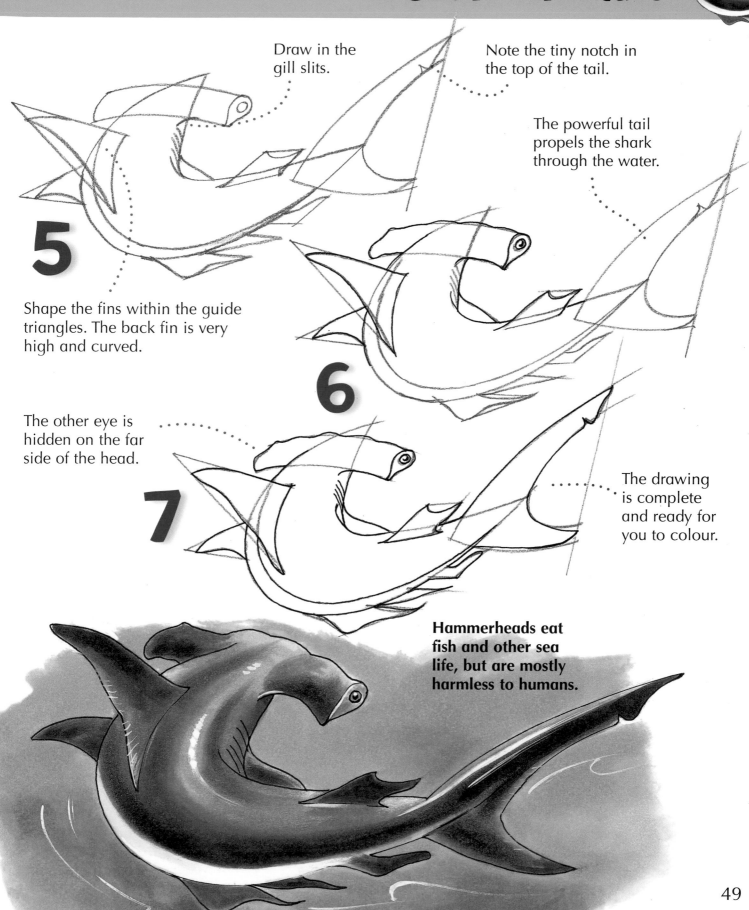

Draw in the gill slits.

Note the tiny notch in the top of the tail.

The powerful tail propels the shark through the water.

5

Shape the fins within the guide triangles. The back fin is very high and curved.

6

The other eye is hidden on the far side of the head.

7

The drawing is complete and ready for you to colour.

Hammerheads eat fish and other sea life, but are mostly harmless to humans.

Sperm Whale

This is the champion deep sea diver. It goes deeper than any other whale (at least 2000 metres) and can stay down for more than an hour before coming up for air. In the depths of the sea, squid are plentiful – and the Sperm Whale eats up to a tonne of squid a day.

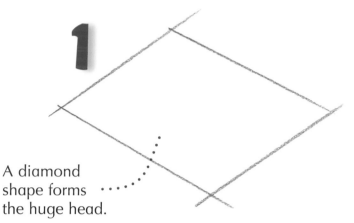

1

A diamond shape forms the huge head.

The head makes up about a third of the total length.

2

Now add a smaller triangle for the tail.

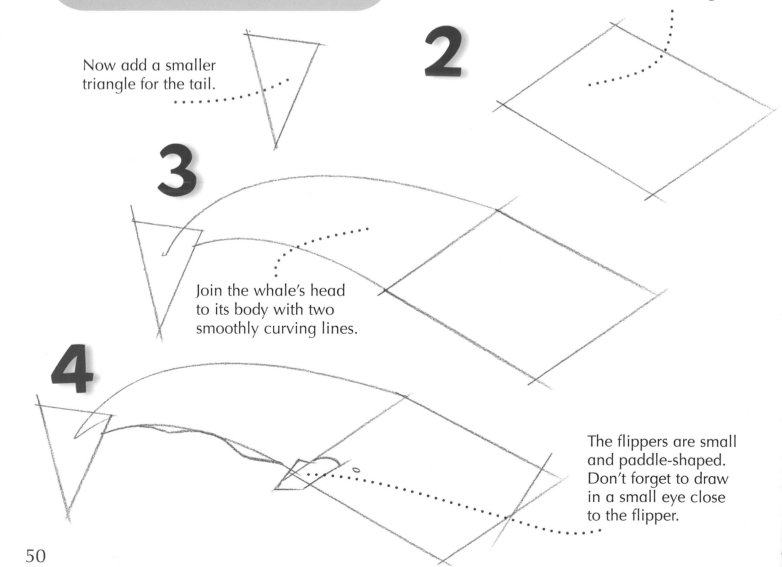

3

Join the whale's head to its body with two smoothly curving lines.

4

The flippers are small and paddle-shaped. Don't forget to draw in a small eye close to the flipper.

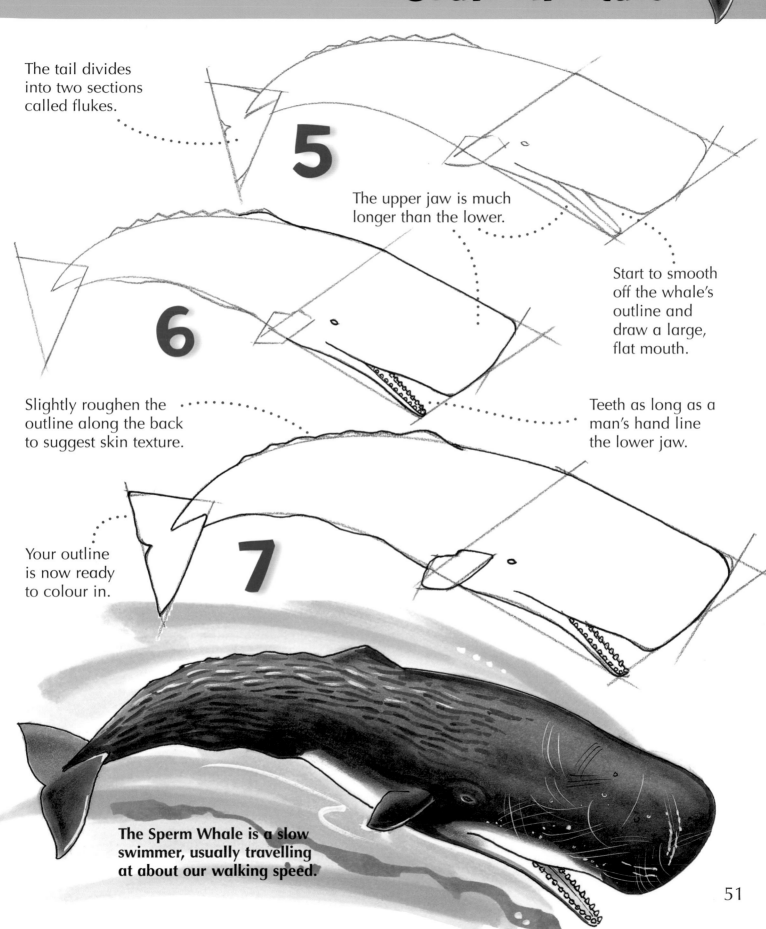

The tail divides into two sections called flukes.

5

The upper jaw is much longer than the lower.

Start to smooth off the whale's outline and draw a large, flat mouth.

6

Slightly roughen the outline along the back to suggest skin texture.

Teeth as long as a man's hand line the lower jaw.

7

Your outline is now ready to colour in.

The Sperm Whale is a slow swimmer, usually travelling at about our walking speed.

Dragonfly

Dragonflies are found all over the world – more than 2500 different kinds of them. In summer they can be seen flashing over ponds and rivers. These are their hunting grounds, where they catch smaller flying insects. Their swift, graceful flight and brilliant colours are eye-catching.

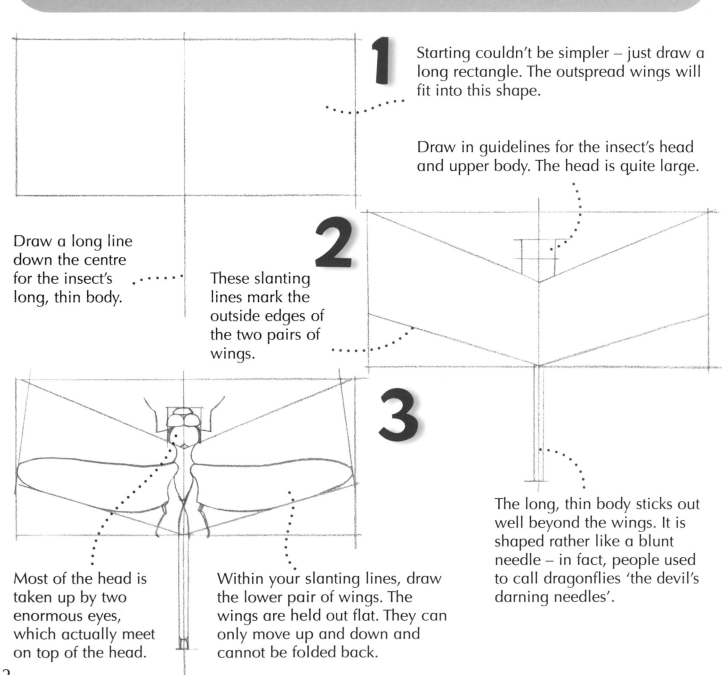

1 Starting couldn't be simpler – just draw a long rectangle. The outspread wings will fit into this shape.

Draw in guidelines for the insect's head and upper body. The head is quite large.

Draw a long line down the centre for the insect's long, thin body.

2 These slanting lines mark the outside edges of the two pairs of wings.

3 The long, thin body sticks out well beyond the wings. It is shaped rather like a blunt needle – in fact, people used to call dragonflies 'the devil's darning needles'.

Most of the head is taken up by two enormous eyes, which actually meet on top of the head.

Within your slanting lines, draw the lower pair of wings. The wings are held out flat. They can only move up and down and cannot be folded back.

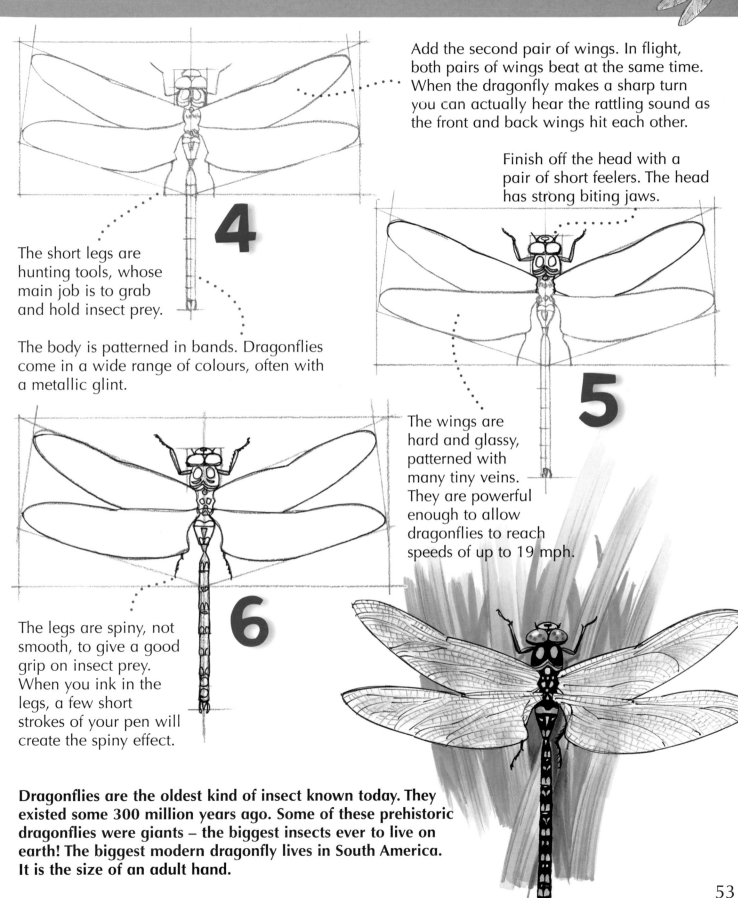

Add the second pair of wings. In flight, both pairs of wings beat at the same time. When the dragonfly makes a sharp turn you can actually hear the rattling sound as the front and back wings hit each other.

Finish off the head with a pair of short feelers. The head has strong biting jaws.

The short legs are hunting tools, whose main job is to grab and hold insect prey.

The body is patterned in bands. Dragonflies come in a wide range of colours, often with a metallic glint.

The wings are hard and glassy, patterned with many tiny veins. They are powerful enough to allow dragonflies to reach speeds of up to 19 mph.

The legs are spiny, not smooth, to give a good grip on insect prey. When you ink in the legs, a few short strokes of your pen will create the spiny effect.

Dragonflies are the oldest kind of insect known today. They existed some 300 million years ago. Some of these prehistoric dragonflies were giants – the biggest insects ever to live on earth! The biggest modern dragonfly lives in South America. It is the size of an adult hand.

Centipede

The name 'centipede' means 'a hundred legs', but that isn't quite right. Different kinds of centipedes may have as many as 170 pairs of legs, or as few as 15 pairs. This tells us at once that the centipede is not a member of the insect family, for all insects have six legs.

1 Start with a simple, long, worm-like shape.

Mark off the end of your 'worm' to form the head, which is distinct from the rest of the body.

2 The last pair of legs are extra long – and extra sensitive, so they work as a pair of extra feelers.

The head bears one pair of longish feelers. The centipede uses these both to taste things and to smell them.

3 Divide the long body up into many short sections, joined together like 'popper' beads.

The first body section contains special poison fangs for killing prey – slugs, insects and worms.

4 Each section of the body carries a pair of legs.

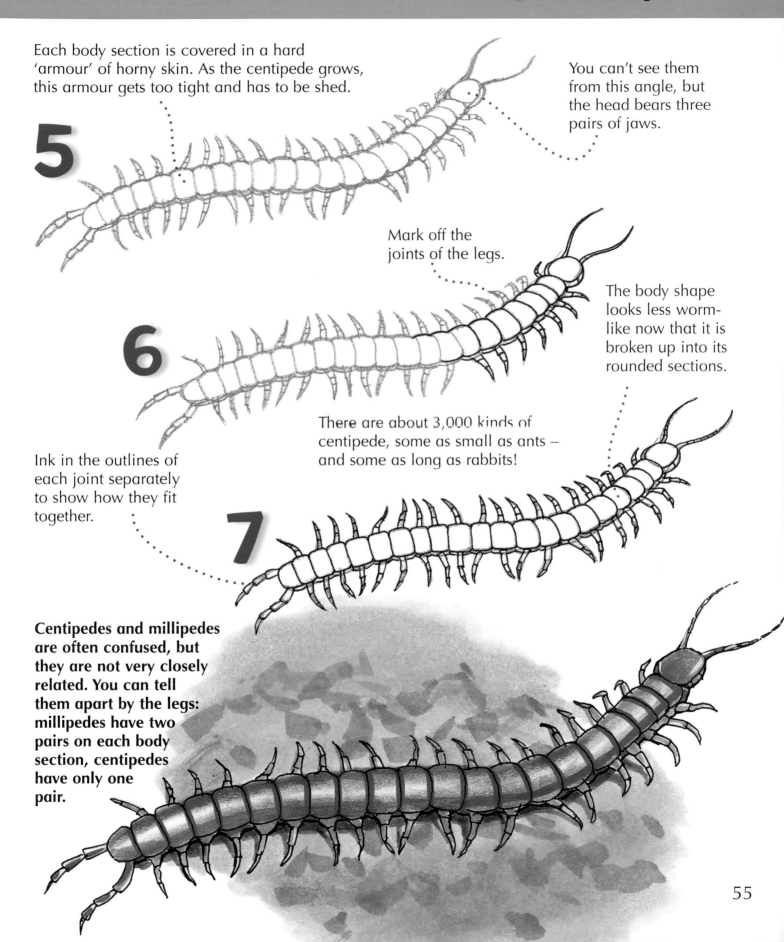

Each body section is covered in a hard 'armour' of horny skin. As the centipede grows, this armour gets too tight and has to be shed.

You can't see them from this angle, but the head bears three pairs of jaws.

5

Mark off the joints of the legs.

The body shape looks less worm-like now that it is broken up into its rounded sections.

6

There are about 3,000 kinds of centipede, some as small as ants – and some as long as rabbits!

Ink in the outlines of each joint separately to show how they fit together.

7

Centipedes and millipedes are often confused, but they are not very closely related. You can tell them apart by the legs: millipedes have two pairs on each body section, centipedes have only one pair.

55

Spider

There are some 40,000 different kinds of spider and they all spin silk. Most weave it into webs to catch insects. Webs range from the well-known round orb webs to simple tubes, complicated funnels, running trip-wires or even, in the case of the bolas spider, a 'lasso' to rope its prey.

These two shapes form the body. Like an insect, a spider's body is in two parts. But, unlike an insect, it has no separate head.

1

2

Add this half-moon shape to mark where the eyes and jaws fit on the front of the body.

Spiders have eight eyes, but as most of them are very short-sighted they rely on their sense of touch.

3

4

Draw lines for the eight legs – another clue that spiders are not insects (which always have six legs).

Build up your lines into legs, marking out the joints. Just like our legs, the top sections are thickest, the lower ones more slender.

This spider has a pattern to break up its colour and help with camouflage.

5

Unlike insects, spiders have no feelers. These two short, leg-like parts at the front of the body are palps, special sensitive mouth-parts, which act rather like feelers.

The silk-spinning organs are found at the back of the body. The silk comes out as a liquid and sets into a fine thread, which the spider then weaves into a web.

6

Most spiders are a dark, dull colour to help them hide away in unlit corners. Some poisonous spiders are brightly coloured, as a warning signal to predators.

Each leg is made up of several tiny sections (you don't need to show all of them!) and ends in tiny claws.

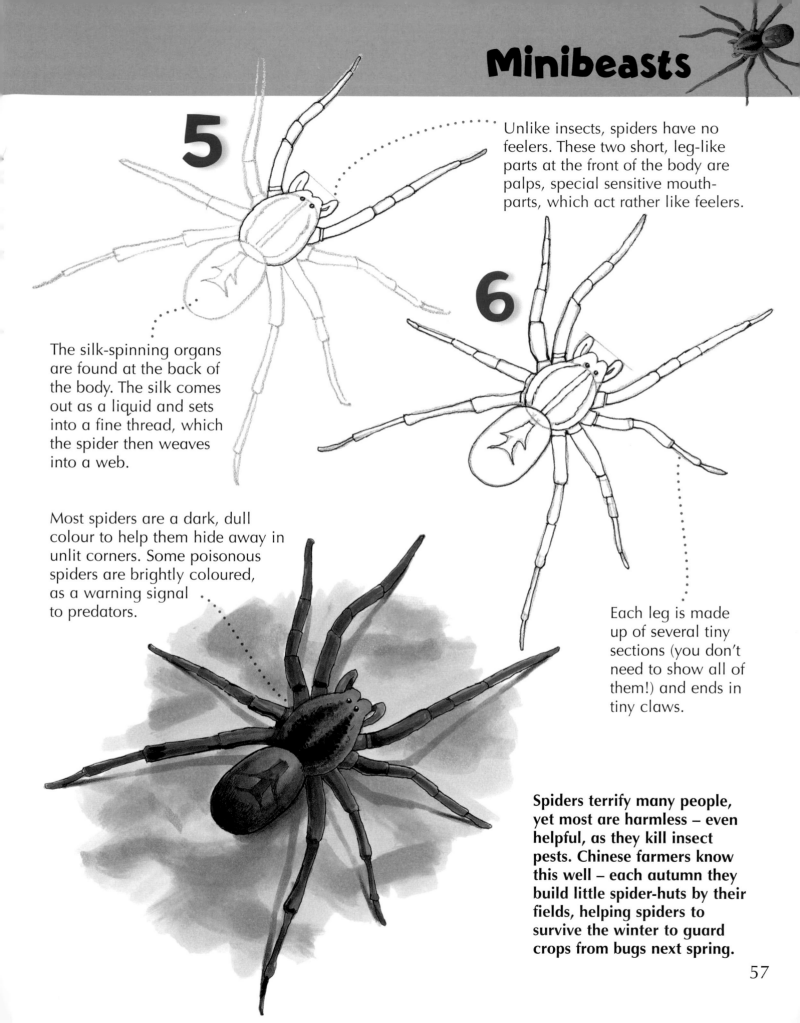

Spiders terrify many people, yet most are harmless – even helpful, as they kill insect pests. Chinese farmers know this well – each autumn they build little spider-huts by their fields, helping spiders to survive the winter to guard crops from bugs next spring.

Wasp

Everybody knows wasps, but not many people like them. They sting and they get into the jam on picnics. But they do have their good points. They kill insect pests, such as flies, and they act as refuse collectors, eating up rubbish such as rotten fruit and decaying flesh.

1

These two simple shapes form the two sections of the body.

2

A big triangle forms guidelines for the upper wing.

The head is fairly large and long, and can turn freely around.

Add two downwards-pointing feelers. These are very sensitive and allow the wasp to smell food from a long way away.

3

Add guidelines for the legs and make a line where the upper wing will end.

Wasps have two pairs of wings. Draw in the pair on this side. The upper wing is bigger than the lower one and provides most of the power for flight.

4

A wasp's body narrows at the point where the two parts join. This is typical of wasps – so we call people with very slender waists 'wasp-waisted'.

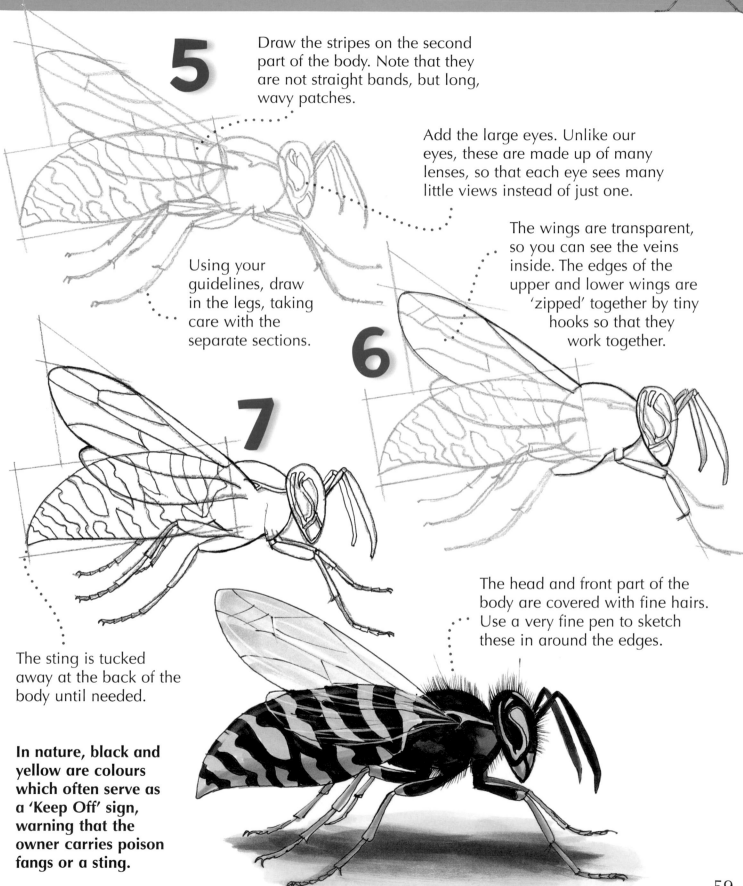

5 Draw the stripes on the second part of the body. Note that they are not straight bands, but long, wavy patches.

Add the large eyes. Unlike our eyes, these are made up of many lenses, so that each eye sees many little views instead of just one.

The wings are transparent, so you can see the veins inside. The edges of the upper and lower wings are 'zipped' together by tiny hooks so that they work together.

Using your guidelines, draw in the legs, taking care with the separate sections.

6

7

The head and front part of the body are covered with fine hairs. Use a very fine pen to sketch these in around the edges.

The sting is tucked away at the back of the body until needed.

In nature, black and yellow are colours which often serve as a 'Keep Off' sign, warning that the owner carries poison fangs or a sting.

Scorpion

Scorpions are deadly hunters with poisoned weapons. Their bodies end in a long 'tail' with a sting at the end. This is used to kill small prey, but it is also for self-defence, so people sometimes get stung. Scorpion stings are very painful and a few are poisonous enough to kill humans.

1

Start at the end, with the curved 'tail' – actually the end of the body.

The 'tail' is held curved over the back, ready to bring its sting into action.

2

Add the front section of the body. Scorpions only have two body parts.

The sting at the end of the 'tail' ends in a fine curved point. It stabs a victim, then injects poison into the wound.

3

These are the tops of four legs, half-hidden by the body. Scorpions have eight legs, like spiders.

These four lines provide a framework for you to draw the large pair of pincers at the front.

4

The pincers look very much like a crab's claws. They are used to seize prey (insects and spiders). They also serve to cut up dinner afterwards.

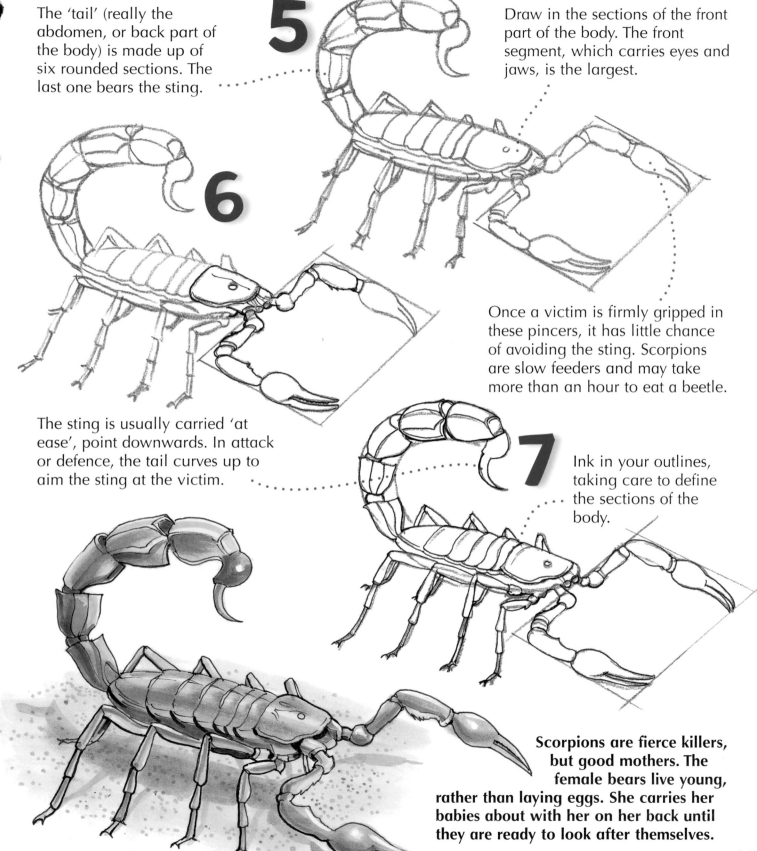

The 'tail' (really the abdomen, or back part of the body) is made up of six rounded sections. The last one bears the sting.

5

Draw in the sections of the front part of the body. The front segment, which carries eyes and jaws, is the largest.

6

Once a victim is firmly gripped in these pincers, it has little chance of avoiding the sting. Scorpions are slow feeders and may take more than an hour to eat a beetle.

The sting is usually carried 'at ease', point downwards. In attack or defence, the tail curves up to aim the sting at the victim.

7

Ink in your outlines, taking care to define the sections of the body.

Scorpions are fierce killers, but good mothers. The female bears live young, rather than laying eggs. She carries her babies about with her on her back until they are ready to look after themselves.

Assassin Bug

We often use the word 'bug' for any creepy crawly. But when scientists talk about bugs they mean a special group of insects with beak-like mouths that stab and suck. This one gets its name of assassin (murderer) from the speed with which it seizes and poisons its victims.

1

These two shapes form the body.

2

Add this shape for the narrow head, which looks too small for the body.

Now draw the feelers, which are even longer than the body and bend downwards at an angle.

Start drawing guidelines for the two hind pairs of legs.

3

The long curving beak of a mouth is used like a hollow needle to stab into the victim's body. It squirts in poison to break down body tissues into a liquid, which it sucks up.

The wings are partly spread, ready to fly. Most of the time they are hidden inside wing-cases, like those of beetles.

4

Now that the beak is in place, you can add the forelegs.

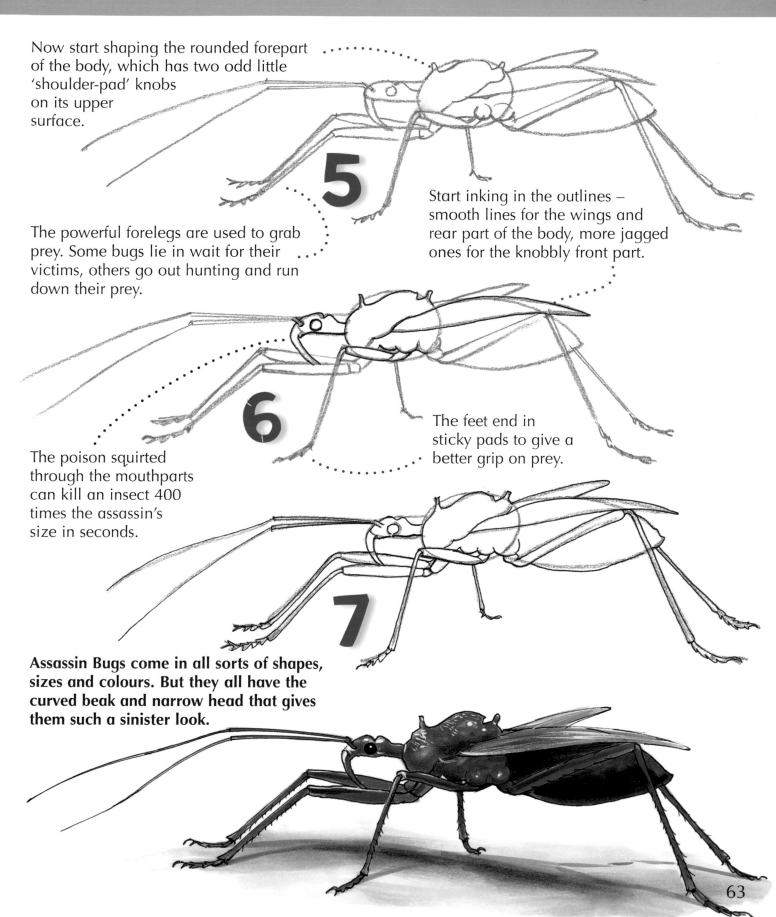

Now start shaping the rounded forepart of the body, which has two odd little 'shoulder-pad' knobs on its upper surface.

5

Start inking in the outlines – smooth lines for the wings and rear part of the body, more jagged ones for the knobbly front part.

The powerful forelegs are used to grab prey. Some bugs lie in wait for their victims, others go out hunting and run down their prey.

6

The feet end in sticky pads to give a better grip on prey.

The poison squirted through the mouthparts can kill an insect 400 times the assassin's size in seconds.

7

Assassin Bugs come in all sorts of shapes, sizes and colours. But they all have the curved beak and narrow head that gives them such a sinister look.

INDEX